MADISON AND ELIJAH

Elijah & His Invisible Friend

written by:
**Sabrena Bishop
and
Elijah Bishop**

illustrated by:
Lionel Emabat

Library of Congress Cataloging-in-Publication Data
Bishop, Sabrena and Bishop, Elijah
Elijah and his invisible friend/ Sabrena Bishop and Elijah Bishop.
Illustration by Lionel Emabat
Summary: A story about a little boy and his dinosaur friend.
ISBN-13: 9781948071130
ISBN-10: 1948071134
Title I. Series. (Volume 1) Bishop Book Series
1. Friendship 2. Dinosaurs
2017958170

Lauren Simone
PUBLISHING HOUSE

This book belongs to:

_____

Dedication

Romae Morgan, Catherine Morgan, Bert St. Amand, and Priscilla Morgan for love, support and valuable feedback.

"Hi Rex! How are you doing today?"

Elijah's mother glanced at him, wondering who he was talking to.

Elijah ran to his room. "Rex, I will get my dump truck and we can dig a big hole."

Mom followed quietly to see what Elijah and his sister, Madison were doing.

"I got the dump truck, Rex. Let's go!" Elijah said excitedly.

"Elijah, my darling, who are you talking to?" Mom asked.

"Mom, I am talking to my friend, Rex. He is a tyrannosaurus. He is large, has green skin, and small eyes." replied Elijah.

"Ok. Copy that!" said Mom. "Just be careful. I know dinosaurs can be dangerous."

"No, Mom! This is my best friend. He won't hurt me."

"Ok, my love. Enjoy!" Mom replied.

"Come on Rex. Let's finish our hole." said Elijah as they ran off together with dump truck to play.

Elijah and Rex played for hours.

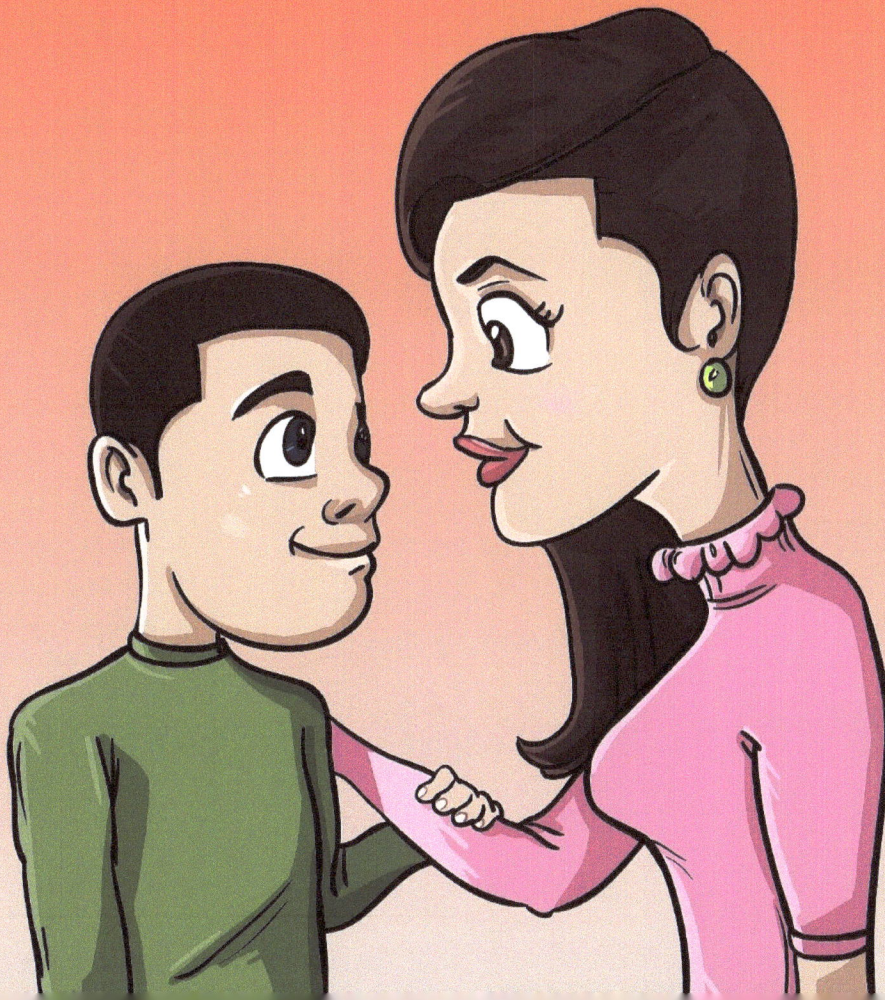

"Did you have fun with Rex?" asked Mom.

"Rex gave me tree leaves to eat and water from the river to drink."

"Rex only eats from the trees and grass, Mom. He doesn't eat chicken or drink soup."

"Sounds like a fun day! Elijah and Madison, it's almost bedtime. Put your toys away, get a snack, and then take your baths!" replied Mom.

"Yes, Mom." answered Madison and Elijah.

"Mom, Rex doesn't like bath time. He's scared of water. So he smells."

Before Elijah's bath, he got a snack. He gave Rex some of his yogurt. Together they ate four yogurts. "Someone's hungry!" said Mom. "Yes, Mom. The tree leaves didn't fill my tummy." Elijah answered.

"Rex, what are you doing tomorrow?" asked Elijah. My birthday party is tomorrow. My friends are coming over to play with me. We will eat ice cream cake."

"Mom will make a lot of food for us to eat. But I don't think you are invited because you are too big. My friends will be scared of you."

"Mom, can Rex come to my party?" asked Elijah. "Well, he could come, but we would have to hide him in the bathroom." said Mom. "That's a good idea, Mom." replied Elijah.

"Rex, I'm going to bed now. We will talk about my party tomorrow. Remember to brush your teeth before you go to sleep."

While Mom read a bedtime story, Elijah fell asleep dreaming about his day with Rex.

DISCUSSION

What was the name of Elijah's friend?

Do you have an invisible friend?

Do you like dinosaurs?

If yes, what is your favorite dinosaur?

FUN FACTS

There are approximately **700 different species** of dinosaurs.

Paleontologists believe there are more species to be discovered.

T-Rex is short for Tyrannosaurus, which means **Tyrant Lizard**.

A T-Rex can sprint up to **20 mph**.

A T-Rex is about **40 feet** (12 meters) tall.

Unlike Rex in the story, T-Rex are known to be **meat lovers**.

VOCABULARY

Carnivore: Animal eater

Dinosaur: An extinct reptile that lived on earth

Extinct: No longer living

Fossil: Preserved life form

Herbivore: Plant eater

Paleontologist: A person who studies extinct life forms and fossil remains

Invisible: A person, animal, or thing that you cannot see with your eyes

Omnivore: Meat and plant eater

Preserve: To keep safe, alive, intact, or prevent from decay, injury, or harm

Terrestrial: Living on earth or land

CREATION STATION

Use playdough to create a dinosaur.

Use toilet paper rolls to create a dinosaur skeleton.

Use a paper plate to create a dinosaur.

On a large sheet of paper, draw and color your favorite dinosaur.

Use an empty tissue box to create T-Rex feet.

ABOUT MADISON & ELIJAH

Madison and Elijah are the children of Sabrena Bishop and Tegarth Bishop. At age 2, Madison's milestone evaluation revealed that Madison's social, motor, and cognitive abilities were developmentally appropriate, but she was delayed for speech. After six months of speech therapy, her mother stopped the sessions and decided to let Madison advance at her own pace. Madison displayed a love of art. At only 6 years old, she has painted over 80 masterpieces. During painting sessions, Madison and Elijah revealed their love for storytelling. Sabrena Bishop contacted Lauren Simone Publishing House to publish their stories. All books are available on Amazon.com, laurensimonepubs.com, and in several book stores.

Follow Madison's and Elijah's journey on Instagram:
@madisonavabishop and **@elijahtheauthor**

www.ingramcontent.com/pod-product-compliance
Lightning Source LLC
Chambersburg PA
CBHW060859270326
41935CB00003B/42